BRITISH POLICY IN THE MIDDLE EAST & THE CREATION OF ISRAEL

ORIGINAL TITLE

AN APPEAL IN BEHALF OF THE JEWISH NATION, IN CONNECTION WITH BRITISH POLICY IN THE LEVANT

By EDWARD L MITFORD ESQ
(CEYLON CIVIL SERVICE)

Laeta et fortia surgunt; quippe solo natura subset

PUBLISHED BY
J. HATCHARD & SON, 187 PICCADILLY, LONDON. 1845

Cover page photograph of dove painted by
Edward Ledwich Mitford FRGS in 1898. The original
painting is on the ceiling of the Mitford Church Bell Tower,
Mitford, Northumberland, England.

MITFORD LITERARY SOCIETY

British Policy in the Middle East and the Creation of Israel.

Original title - An Appeal in Behalf of the Jewish Nation, in connection with British Policy in the Levant by E.L.Mitford. Published by J. Hatchard & Son, 187 Piccadilly. London 1845.

This edition published in 2015 by the Mitford Literary Society Email address - mitford@orange.fr

ISBN – 13: 9781515087830
ISBN – 10: 1515087832

Cover page photograph of dove painted by Edward Ledwich Mitford FRGS in 1898. The original painting is on the ceiling of the Mitford Church Bell Tower, Mitford, Northumberland, England. Edward was elected Fellow of the Royal Geographic Society on 23rd April 1883.

Cover photograph -

Also on Facebook – Mitford Literary Society

MITFORD LITERARY SOCIETY

Edward Ledwich Mitford FRGS (1811-1912) lived to be over 100 years of age through the reigns of six sovereigns. He was 4 years old during the Battle of Waterloo and educated in Paris, France and excelled in languages, including French, German and Arabic. At the age of 18 years he became British Consul in Morocco until 1835. He then travelled 7000 miles on horseback, across 16 countries from London to Ceylon and became the British Consul in Colombo, Sri Lanka. In his time he was a specialist on the Middle East and wrote several fascinating books covering its people and culture. On retirement he succeeded to the family estates in Mitford, Northumberland and Hunmanby and Filey Bay in Yorkshire. Two of his sons, two grandsons and one great grandson went on to become squires and owners of Mitford Castle and estates. His youngest son Bertram Mitford FRGS became a well known author, writing 43 bestselling novels covering the culture and history of South Africa. Edward also served on the bench of Newcastle magistrate's court for many years. The remarkable story of his life follows in the book entitled The Mitford Dynasty to be published in due course.

MITFORD LITERARY SOCIETY

 Hugh Mitford Raymond is the great-great grandson of Edward Ledwich Mitford and nephew and cousin to the last seven squires of Mitford Castle on the direct mainline of the Mitford family of Mitford, Northumberland since 1042. Born and bred in South Africa, Hugh grew up on the back of a horse and later went on to train and breed racehorses. He has served in the South African Defence Force completing active duties in Mozambique, Caprivi Strip and South West Africa. He also managed large farming operations in Zimbabwe. He speaks four languages and has travelled the world, including the Middle East, working for various international companies, along with IBM and United Nations. He has been resident in the South of France for the past 20 years. He is a member of the London Society of Authors, National Union of Journalists and Chairman of the South African International Association of the Riviera. The synopsis of his first book The Mitford Dynasty, to be published next year follows at the back of this book.

MITFORD LITERARY SOCIETY

Foreword

This book was written over 150 years ago before the current Israeli-Palestinian conflict. In the middle of the 19th century, colonization was in full swing with the European powers quarrelling and dividing up the distant lands around the world.

Amidst the building of the British Empire and its carving up of lands and oceans to establish colonies around the world - there followed the abolition of slavery and the rise of the oppressed with the start of their movements and causes to establish recognition and a fair deal. With wars and conflict and continuing political unrest only a few politicians knew the real meaning of altruism apart from personal graft and endeavour.

However, there was one person that chose to do things differently. Perhaps his dash of Irish blood, his humble and engaging nature and his excellent way with life?

As a young man, he spent over 5 years in Morocco and it's here in Mogador where he first experienced the most horrendous scenes of violence against the Jews that marked his mind forever. They were subjected to trial – by the mob and simply burnt alive.

Much later for his job he chose to travel on horseback from London to Ceylon, to places where no European had been before – through all the countries of the East – Arabia and India. What's known as the Middle East today. Of everything he experienced and witnessed was the consistent aggression and violence towards a certain group of people who had no way or ability to defend themselves. The Jews were stateless and anti-Semitism was everywhere.

His life and work is part of English history and cannot continue to be hidden from public knowledge. He was the first British government high official to present a plan to the British government – well before Herzl, Balfour or Ben Gourion and before the Zionist movement took form in Switzerland in 1897, to share Palestine with one of the most creative and industrious people in Europe.

This man, Edward Ledwich Mitford, was the patriarch of one of the oldest families of England. His ancient castle in Northumberland, near the borders of England and Scotland was never rebuilt and remains a ruin, but his legacy is vast and the Mitford family numerous, with writers, politicians, financiers ...around the world.

During his journey he kept a detailed diary of his experiences and travels, day after day, which provides the reason for presenting what is to follow.

The publisher (editor) of this book is none other than his great-great grandson, a native of South Africa, and the author of a biography of the Mitford Dynasty to appear soon. The reason he has republished the work of his great-great grandfather is purely historical and far from any debate. Obviously, times have changed, the situation in the Middle East is not any more the same but the text reveals the mentalities of the time and certain philosophies and the festering germs of later decisions.

Some terms have been modified for a better understanding of the text, without distorting or altering the initial intent. The publisher (editor) does not take a stand and only wishes to deliver a historic testimony of a project which anchors in time much of the current events even today. This book allows the reader to better understand the reasons of British presence in the Middle East, its politics and policy, its diplomacy, its implication and the responsibilities in the conflicts to come over a land promised to two peoples - so different yet so similar.

Finally, the reader will not miss to draw a parallel between Edward Mitford and his quest to provide a homeland for the Jewish nation to the pro Nazi and fascist commitments of Diana and Unity Mitford, two of the famous and infamous Mitford sisters. Diana divorced Bryan Guinness of the Guinness Brewery fortune to marry Sir Oswald Mosley, leader of the British Union of Fascists and Unity became intimately involved with Hitler and his anti-Semitic ideas until her failed attempt at committing suicide, when Hitler sent her back to England via Switzerland.

Jean-Laurent Durrand

Avant-propos

Ce livre a été écrit voilà plus de 150 ans à une époque où le conflit israélo-palestinien n'avait pas encore fait parler de lui mais où certains s'interrogeaient déjà sur le droit des juifs à disposer d'une terre.

Au milieu de ce 19ème siècle, la colonisation est en plein essor. Les états européens se disputent et se partagent les richesses de terres plus ou moins lointaines, établissent des comptoirs, des établissements, des colonies partout dans le monde.

Dans ce contexte de partage du monde, des terres comme des océans, de nombreux peuples sont opprimés ou soumis ; certains connaissent l'esclavage ou subissent des déplacements... La question du peuple juif à la recherche d'une terre pour s'établir commence à poindre mais n'intéresse encore guère. Ce seront la montée des nationalismes et de l'antisémitisme en Europe qui feront naitre un mouvement sioniste visant à créer un État pour les Juifs, ravivant ainsi d'anciennes mais vivaces velléités, et dont 1948 verra l'avènement.

Mais, en ce milieu du 19ème siècle, il en est certains qui, ayant voyagé à travers l'Orient, témoins de scènes antisémites violentes, ont été sensibilisés à la cause de juifs, pour certains apatrides, rejetés ou exclus, soumis à l'oppression et à la vindicte populaire pour des raisons religieuses.

Parmi ceux-ci, il en est un dont l'Histoire n'a guère retenu le nom mais qui pourtant peut être considéré comme le premier ayant établi un plan de partage de la Palestine dans le but d'offrir aux juifs opprimés une terre à eux, et ce bien avant Herzl, Balfour ou Ben Gourion.

Cet homme, Edward Ledwich Mitford, est un aristocrate, patriarche d'une des plus anciennes familles d'Angleterre, sinon la plus ancienne, dont le château, au nord du Northumberland, près de la frontière avec l'Ecosse, n'est plus que ruine depuis des siècles, mais dont le domaine est immensément vaste et les Mitford se rencontrent dans tous les domaines de la vie civile ou militaire.

E.L. Mitford visite le monde. Il travaille à Mogador au Maroc où des scènes de violence contre les juifs le marquent à jamais. Ensuite, il se rend à Ceylan, à cheval, depuis Londres. C'est durant ce périple qui le mène en Asie Mineure, au proche et moyen Orient, en Mésopotamie et jusqu'aux Indes qu'il rédige jour après jour des courriers et des notes qui une fois compilées formeront ce livre.

Son éditeur aujourd'hui n'est autre que son arrière arrière petit-fils, natif d'Afrique du Sud, auteur d'une biographie des Mitford à paraître prochainement. C'est dans un seul but historique, loin de toute polémique, qu'il a souhaité exhumer et publier à nouveau le travail de son ancêtre. Evidemment, les temps ont changé, la situation au Proche-Orient n'est plus la même mais le texte est révélateur des mentalités de l'époque, d'une certaine philosophie et porte en lui les germes des décisions de partage futures. Quelques termes ont dû être modifiés pour une meilleure compréhension du texte, sans en altérer le fond. L'éditeur ne prend aucun parti et souhaite seulement livrer un témoignage historique d'un projet qui s'ancre dans l'époque mais reste ô combien d'actualité encore aujourd'hui. Il permet aussi de mieux comprendre les raisons de la présence britannique dans cette région du monde, sa politique, sa diplomatie, son implication sinon ses responsabilités dans les conflits à venir sur une terre promise à deux peuples aussi différents que semblables et que tout semble opposer... et rapprocher.

Enfin, le lecteur ne manquera pas de faire un parallèle entre E.L. Mitford, décidé à donner aux juifs la terre de leurs ancêtres, et l'engagement pronazi et fasciste de Diana et Unity Mitford, deux des fameuses sulfureuses sœurs Mitford, issues d'une branche de la famille. Diana épousa la cause fasciste en même temps que son leader, Oswald Mosley, et Unity fut si proche des idées anti-sémites d'Hitler qu'elle en devint sa maîtresse avant de tenter de se suicider.

Jean-Laurent Durrand

MITFORD LITERARY SOCIETY

PREFACE

Hidden historical secrets from the Mitford family archives.

In his book "The Vision Was There - A History of the British Movement for the Restoration of the Jews to Palestine", Franz Kobler writes of my great-great grandfather Edward Ledwich Mitford F.R.G.S. This book shows the trends in British thinking that gave rise to the Restoration Movement that resulted in the British Mandate over Palestine from which emerged the State of Israel.

"In 1845, two high colonial officials Edward Ledwich Mitford and Colonel Gawler, presented two opposite political opinions which were to set the course of history as we know it today. Edward Mitford stood for the establishment of a Jewish State, while Gawler distrusted such "wild schemes" and recommended the colonization of Palestine as part of the Turkish Empire". Edward published a book "An Appeal in Behalf of the Jewish Nation in connection with British Policy in the Levant" in 1845, published by J. Hatchard & Son, Piccadilly, London. His plan ultimately led to the Balfour Declaration of 2 November 1917. As you will read, a branch of the Mitford family would turn full circle within the British and European Jewish community.

In this book, Edward Mitford, one of Lord Palmerston's colleagues' (Palmerston served as both Foreign Secretary and Prime Minister) in the Foreign Service, highlighted his opinion of the Jewish people possessing the qualities of "fortitude and perseverance" being responsible for the miracle of their continuity. For this remarkable and creative people, Edward Mitford demanded an independent State. Up until this time there had never been a state in Palestine, an Arab State, a Muslim Sate or a Palestinian State. Britain was not in the business of making nations and countries but rather wanted to ensure continued stability and economic continuity and control for its long term strategic protection of its trade route to India and the opening of the Suez Canal in 1869. Edward was one of the very few British government officials who had an intimate, detailed and documented knowledge of Palestine and the Middle East countries and fluent in all the Arab dialects.

"The plan I would propose is, first, the establishment of the Jewish nation in Palestine, as a protected state, under the guardianship of Great Britain, secondly their final establishment, as an independent State, when the parent institutions shall have acquired sufficient force and vigour to allow this tutelage being withdrawn..."

With the various waves of settlers arriving in Palestine (likewise in South Africa and other British colonies) from the early 1820's, Edward Mitford very astutely was quick to highlight the dilemma of the indigenous population and their attitude towards Jewish immigrants - his statement was very relevant. "The country, compared with its size, is at present thinly populated, yet the pressure caused by the introduction of so large a body of strangers upon the actual inhabitants might be attended with injurious results. Before attempting to make a settlement it would be desirable that the country should be prepared for their reception.

This might be done by inducing the Turkish government to make the local inhabitants fall back upon the extensive and partially cultivated countries of Asia Minor, where they might be put in possession of tracts and allocations, equally advantageous and far superior in value to those they abandoned". These early settlers had to carve out their existence and living from the barren and rocky lands, which later led to the kibbutz programme and creation of employment and agricultural projects, continued to this day.

In the build up to his plan Edward's book also includes a synopsis of his previous book "An Arab's Pledge – A Tale of Morocco" which presents factual evidence of the cultural differences between the Muslim and Jewish cultures portrayed through the brutal killing of an innocent Jewish girl.

As you will read in the pages ahead in his own words, the introduction to his book starts off as follows. "The purpose of this book is three-fold. Firstly – to expose the injustice and cruelty which the Jewish nation endures, especially at the hands of the Arabs. Secondly, to appeal to the British people and the ministers of the British Empire, in their behalf, and thirdly to point out how England may remedy the evils complained of, and at the same time very considerably promote the strength of her political position and the prosperity of her colonial dependencies. The direct religious question is avoided as much as possible.

The time is right for mighty changes and whatever events may happen, will be brought about by the natural course of providence". He leaves the reader to form his own judgement and decision. His appeal goes on to state the practicalities and process of achieving an independent state with regards to worldwide opinion, the position of Russia and other European countries and their influence in the Middle east. Edward died five years before the Balfour Declaration of 2 November 1917. Everything detailed in Edward's book and the plan he laid out in 1845 took place and happened, it set the framework for the British mandate that followed in 1920-1948.

There were other great luminaries who devoted their minds to the Jewish cause. Theodor Herzl presented "The Jewish State" in 1896. A year later he hosted the first world Zionist congress in Switzerland and as a result established the World Zionist Organisation. Its aim was to create a legal home in Palestine for the Jewish nation. Then there was Chaim Weizmann, a Russian Jew, who captivated the British with his scientific mind and inventions. He had discovered a process for making ingredients to develop explosives which naturally elevated him into the upper echelons of the British government. He later went on to raise millions for the Jewish cause and became President of the Zionist Organization and was the first President of Israel from 1949 until his death in 1952. It was Weizmann that linked the USA with the newly formed state of Israel. Weizmann became the centre of British foreign policy and charmed Arthur Balfour with his vision of Israel.

After the Sykes–Picot Agreement in 1916 – a secret agreement between the United Kingdom and France, with the assent of Russia, dividing up the Ottoman Empire (also known as the Asia Minor Agreement) – Foreign Secretary, Arthur James Balfour sent the following letter to Baron Rothschild in regard to the establishment of a national home in Palestine for the Jewish people.

"His Majesty's government views with favour the establishment in Palestine of a national home for the Jewish people, and will use their best endeavours to facilitate the achievement of this object, it being clearly understood that nothing shall be done which may prejudice the civil and religious rights of existing non-Jewish communities in Palestine, or the rights and political status enjoyed by Jews in any other country".

As stated by Uri Avnery - famous for crossing the lines during the Siege of Beirut to meet Yasser Arafat on 3 July 1982, the first time the Palestinian leader ever met with an Israeli. Avnery is the author of several books about the Israeli-Palestinian conflict. His synopsis of the Balfour Declaration is as follows; "It put Zionism on the political map. It was an alliance between British imperialism and Zionism which both sides gained from. The Balfour Declaration was a British ruse to take away Palestine from the French who got Syria – Palestine was part of Syria historically and Palestine would have fallen to the Syrians without the Balfour Declaration. The British needed Palestine to bring the oil from Mosul to Haifa and safeguard the Suez Canal and their gateway to India. Together with the League of Nations it was an excellent deal, except the British pulled out".

Edward was a recognized specialist on the Middle East - actively engaged in British foreign policy and intimate friends with all the leading politicians including Sir Moses Montefiore, President of the Jewish Board of Deputies for 28 years. Little did he know that some years later in the 1930's the British Labour Party politician, Sir Oswald Mosley, (a potential candidate for Prime Minister) would establish a new party called the British Union of Fascists, which claimed the Jews were leading Britain to war?

In addition Unity Mitford became an intimate friend of Adolf Hitler and openly publicized herself as a "Jew hater", reported throughout the British and international press. In fact most of Lord and Lady Redesdale's, or the Freeman-Mitford family and children, the Mitford girls… became Nazi, fascist and communist sympathizers. Diana Mitford having married Bryan Guinness, heir to the Guinness brewery fortune, several years later fell in love with Sir Oswald Mosley, leader of the British Union of Fascists. They married in secret while staying with Joseph and Magda Goebbels with Adolf Hitler as witness. Based on her older sister Nancy's testimony, Diana and Sir Oswald spent three years in Holloway prison. We think it was due to their project to set up a radio broadcasting station between Germany and England. A third sister, Jessica, became a communist and emigrated to America. According to my parents and during the post war years – the family, uncles and cousins took a long time to get over this, if at all. Quite some baggage to lump around?

On retirement, Edward L Mitford became the 27th Squire of Mitford, Northumberland and at the grand old age of 85 years inherited Mitford Castle and estates without a penny in the bank, except his annual government pension. His two oldest sons went on to inherit the family estates in Northumberland and Yorkshire and the third son Bertram (a friend of Rider Haggard, Rudyard Kipling and Cecil John Rhodes and others) wrote 43 bestselling novels covering the early history of South Africa. The story of Edward, Bertram and many other amazing, charming and crazy members of the Mitford family is contained in a new book entitled "The Mitford Dynasty" to be published in due course. A synopsis follows at the back of this book.

According to Franz Kobler, Edward L Mitford may well be considered the forerunner of the trend which supported the renaissance of the Jewish nation in the Land of Israel on grounds very similar to the principles of Judaism itself. Here follows Edwards's historical appeal in behalf of the Jewish Nation written in 1845, presented by his great-great grandson exactly 170 years later.

Hugh Mitford Raymond
France 2015

References

Zionism & the British Empire - Stephen P Meyer 2009
An Appeal in behalf of the Jewish Nation by Edward Ledwich Mitford 1845
Tranquillisation of Syria and the East: Observations and Practical
Suggestions, George Gawler 1845
The Vision Was There. A History of the British Movement for the
Restoration of the Jews to Palestine by Franz Kobler, originally published
by the World Jewish Congress 1956

AN APPEAL IN BEHALF OF THE JEWISH NATION, IN CONNECTION WITH BRITISH POLICY IN THE MIDDLE EAST

This book was written in Colombo, Ceylon, now Sri Lanka in 1845. Based on my great-great grandfathers firsthand knowledge and his many years of experience in the Middle East countries, as detailed in his books entitled "The Arabs Pledge" and "A Land March from England to Ceylon", you'll readily appreciate his moral fibre, his humble nature and exquisite understanding of all the Middle Eastern people, tribes and cultures during his time. The writer born in Africa, generations later, spent time working in the Middle East and gained an insight to this - a culture totally and completely different to the westernized mind and way of life. We can learn, and when we learn – we can understand and appreciate both western and Arab cultures. As Edward did – and it's his understanding, set out in this book that motivated and developed the framework leading to the creation of the country of ISRAEL.

Hugh

July 2015

MITFORD LITERARY SOCIETY

INTRODUCTION by EDWARD MITFORD FRGS

The purpose of the writer is three-fold. Firstly - to expose the injustice and cruelty which the Jewish nation still endures, especially at the hands of the Arabs. Secondly - to appeal to the British people and the ministers of the British Empire, on their behalf. And thirdly - to point out how England may remedy the evils complained of and at the same time very considerably, promote the strength of her political position and the prosperity of her colonial dependencies.

The direct religious question is avoided as much as possible and my object is not to excite the emotions, or stir up the passions, but to direct, I presume, and not to determine, the readers mind and judgement.

The time appears ripe for the accomplishment of mighty changes. The author, however, avows his impression, that whatever events may happen, they will be brought about by the apparent ordinary course of Providence. And of late years, all things have swept onward with such silent yet fearful velocity, that they might almost be supernatural. It is that Great Britain may have the privilege of being the instrument of God's providence towards the Jewish Nation, which has partly influenced the proposer of the following plan. It is recommended by the facts which he has had the opportunity of verifying.

He has resided and travelled for many years in the Middle East, and the countries of Central Asia, and has everywhere met with many Jewish people who are spread over the habitable globe. Of the feasibility of the proposition which is here suggested, he now leaves the reader to form his own judgement and decision.

E. Mitford

Colombo, March 1845.

EDWARD'S APPEAL TO THE BRITISH GOVERNMENT

We look abroad into the world and we behold the nations of Europe in the enjoyment of all the blessings of civilization derived from the wonderful advance of knowledge and science which have recently poured in, as it were, like a flood upon the western portion of the globe. The people of the East have derived reflected advantages from the same cause. There is an evident amelioration in their institutions. The spirit of peace more generally pervades the present races (see Note 1 page 40) and promises greater fruits of the same spirit to the rising generations and they are in a great measure freed from the inhibiting constraints of superstition and tyranny.

But while the British statesmen freely offer the pledge of the nation's honour and contributes her wealth to the utter eradication of slavery – while England waves her protecting banner over the helpless and the oppressed both at home and overseas – there yet remains one nation – one remarkable race of people – the Jews – towards whom the exercise of philanthropy would seem a crime – whom no eye pities and whose wretched condition is a stain upon the present age of the world, worthy only of the darkness, blindness and inhumanity of the Middle Ages.

I am aware that much of the ill-feeling of former times against this hapless nation has been greatly effaced from English hearts but much prejudice still exists even in enlightened England. In other countries of Europe this feeling amounts to positive hatred - but it can be remembered, the Christian world despises these people for vices which have been fostered by itself - and it hates them for crimes which are the effects of its own heartless policy.

Let not some arch-priest or Levite (historically they were assistants to the Temple priests and of the tribe of Levi) of selfishness passing by on the other side tell me that the curse of the Most High is on the Jewish race and that to help them would be to contravene the purposes of God's providence. Was this not their cry, when, despite the hypocrisy, the nation arose as one man and hurled from the height of the pure cliffs of Albion the iron shackles of the children of Ham, redeemed with gold of its sons, into everlasting depths of its native seas?

The curse of slavery was upon the Negro – as the curse of oppression is upon the Jew – but it was not considered a reason because we could not entirely remove that curse, that we should not do our utmost to mitigate it and at least wash our hands of its guilt. Judas was not innocent although his Master must needs betrayed, neither shall we be guiltless instruments in the oppression of our brethren, if we do not our utmost to mitigate their sufferings – of this, indeed we have positive assurance – as well might the Samaritan have looked on his neighbour as suffering under the dispensations of Providence and so excused himself as we can plead their curse in extenuation of our uncharitableness and neglect of duty.

But besides the unanswerable arguments of humanity and Christian duty, we know not how far we may be the honoured instruments of the restoration of the Jewish culture and their place among the nations. This subject has latterly been more forcibly impressed on my mind by the outrages perpetrated on the Jews of Mogadore, consequent on its occupation by the French, who, however, were blameless of any participation in them.

I was connected with Mogadore (Essaouira) on the Atlantic coast and other parts of the dominions of Morocco for upwards of five years and had thus an opportunity of becoming intimately acquainted with the state of the very large section of the Jewish people who are spread through its various towns. They are a fine race and are partly the descendants of those Jews who were banished by the Christian rulers of Europe from their several dominions and forced to take refuge in the adjacent Arab countries where they enjoyed at least a precarious protection, preferable to the state of being outlaws, trembling in fear of Christian Europe.

It's needless to enter into the details of the atrocities practised towards this unprotected nation in Spain and other European countries for so many centuries. They are familiar to all... they stand forth as dark monuments on the pages of history, as prominent as the massacres of Alva, the black deeds of the unholy inquisition (with which these were connected), or the horrors of the French revolution... but it is not foreign to the subject to remark, in the way of warning that the decline and downfall to its present state of anarchy of the Spanish nation is easily and naturally traced, being mainly attributable (second only to the just retribution of Providence) to the persecution and banishment from her soil of this wealthy, intelligent, industrious and unoffending race.

These outcasts of Europe flying for refuge to the Barbary shores, met and amalgamated with the stream of Israelitish wanderers from the eastward who had escaped the torrent of Arab invasion and the proselytising sword of Mohammed; these indeed were only a remnant as whole towns of Jews in the north of Africa were compelled to embrace Islamism. There is an instance of this in the city of Fez, whose inhabitants and particularly the women are celebrated for their beauty and fairness, which they derive from their Hebrew blood. They are stated by traditional history to have been all Jews, when the march of the conquering hordes spread desolation over these beautiful provinces and this city embraced the alternative of apostasy to escape the sword.

In the towns of Morocco alone there are 30,000 Jews who enjoy the same protection that their fathers enjoyed from the Moslem sultans, but no more – for the Moslem Arab is unchangeable and un-progressive. (Throughout the Barbary States there are over 1,000,000 Jews). The same waves of oppression roll over them now as formerly; their condition is not absolutely changed for the worse; though it is so, compared with the general amelioration around them. Their heaven is still brass and their earth iron.

Not blinded like the Spaniard, the Moor knows their value and although he holds them in the direst bondage, he will not allow them to escape his grasp by leaving the country of their oppressors. Morocco, while it is the nearest to Europe of any of the Barbary States, is the farthest removed from the influence of science and civilization and a description of their position in this country will show, with slight modification, the position they hold in most Muslim states. Cowardice and avarice are inculcated into them with the first dawn of intellect: their spirit is broken even in childhood.

Their children are the fairest and most lovely I have ever seen, their faces beaming with health and intelligence and the independent spirit of the man strong and budding within them; but how soon does all this promise disappear under the training of their parents, whom stern necessity has taught that their only safety lies in the contempt of their rulers which they therefore study to incur by the most abject servility. I have watched these children and I know nothing more painful than to witness this crushing of the spirit of a child of nobles and generous promise to suit the baseness of its future lot, except it be to see the father trembling at some incautious bursting forth of yet unseared feeling or childish independence in the presence of their masters; the consequence is, that their minds are warped to obloquy and degradation and their features early mould themselves to the obliquity of their souls. Yet under different treatment and a more fostering hand, they have still the latent qualities of the stock of which Abraham and David, Joshua and the Asmoneans, and the apostles of Christ, who himself condescended in the flesh to be of this nation and people.

But let us look to the state of bondage of which this moral degradation is the fruit. This large body of Jews scattered through Morocco has in each town its separate quarter walled in, at the gates of which a guard is stationed every night: they are forbidden to possess arms of any kind: they are compelled to wear a distinctive and degrading dress, the chief articles of which are a black felt cap and black shoes, and the latter must always be taken off and carried in the hand on passing a mosque, or other sacred building, a town-gate or the residence of any person of rank, and also before governors or persons in authority: they are not allowed to ride horses; nor even donkeys or mules, within towns or in sight of any mosque or sanctuary.

They are obliged to do any work required of them by an Arab and to bear the grossest abuse and insults without a murmur. Even the right of self defence is taken from them, for if a Jew raises his hand against a Moor, although smarting under aggravated insults and even more blows, the penalty is amputation of the offending hand. A Moslem can enter a Jew's house and compel him to furnish whatever he may call for, whilst the owner of the house is too glad to buy his forbearance on such easy terms, and is fortunate if his women are not insulted and himself spurned. No compunction is felt in taking their lives and such is the abject contempt in which they are held that the Moors do not scruple to admit them to the apartments of their own females and if this deviation from their usual jealous custom is noticed or remarked on, they tell you an expression of surprise that "they are only Jews" implying that they do not look on them even as men.

The richer Jews are the bankers and agents of the men of consequence who are either alkaïds or officers of rank in the sultan's service and invariably, when these men die, the unfortunate Jew who is their agent is mulcted in a large amount, under pretext that he was owing to the deceased, and at his death devolved on the government: the evidence of account books and witnesses are equally laughed at and disregarded and the unanswerable arguments of the bastinado, chains and imprisonment, exercised on frames accustomed to luxury and ease, extort the gold, whether or not, from their reluctant grasp.

One of the most diabolical means of oppression which is brought to bear on this condemned race, but of which fortunately the instances are comparatively few, arises primarily from the contempt with which they are regarded; their evidence being esteemed utterly worthless before the tribunal of the caadi against a Moslem, while the evidence of two Moslem witnesses (though often false) is sufficient to convict a Jew and subject him to the penalty of the grossest crimes. It will easily be perceived how this unlimited power can be applied to the purposes of avarice, sensuality and religious bigotry, when taken in connection with the fact that nothing more is required to make a Jew or a Christian a Moslem by their law, than the deposition of two witnesses to the simple circumstance of their having pronounced the words "There is no God but God, and Mohammed is the apostle of God". Against this testimony the protestations of the Jew are in vain and the penalty of recantation is burning at the stake.

Although the instances, as I before mentioned are few, this is too great a power not to be much too frequently used for the worst purposes; sometimes the threat is sufficient to gain the proposed end, but if that fails, false witnesses are employed when the victim, who is generally wealthy, purchases immunity at a ruinous price, and the circumstance is hushed up; or if poor, which is seldom, he is obliged to conform to his new faith, hated by his own people and despised and always suspected by his adopted brethren.

Some cases are, however, attended by circumstances of a graver nature, and have a more tragical ending. One of them I will narrate, which took place while I was in that country and with which I was well acquainted. The individual sufferer was an interesting young Jewess of respectable family, residing at Tangier and much is it to be regretted that our consul-general had not influence, or if he did possess any, that he did not exert it to avert the horrid catastrophe. This young girl was summoned before the tribunal of the caadi by two Moors who deposed to her having pronounced their confession of faith. This, however, she utterly denied, but, as before shown, in vain, and the caadi had no alternative, even had he possessed the inclination, but to decree her conformity to Islam on pain of death.

I was never able to obtain correct information as to whether the witnesses were actuated by sinister motives, or whether the poor girl really did repeat the fatal words in jest. There is doubtless much friendly intercourse existing between Jews and the better disposed Moors, in which gossip and jesting are sometimes carried beyond the verge of safety, considering the relative position of the parties. Again, in a scriptural language like the Arabic, in which the name God so constantly occurs, there are many ejaculations repeatedly uttered by the Jews which approach very near to this formula and might therefore be mistaken for it. Be this as it may, the affair was of too serious a nature to be passed over lightly by the Jewish community, who at least deserve the credit of uniting for mutual protection, where their national and religious integrity are concerned and consequently every exertion was made but unsuccessfully, by influence and money, to crush it in the bud. It had, however, become too public not to reach the ears of Mulai Abderahman, to whose decision it was therefore referred and the parties repaired to Fez for the purpose.

Whatever might have influenced her accusers, there could be no doubt of the motive of the sultan in enforcing the decree, which was to obtain another plaything for his harem; in fact, so well known was his character in this respect, that from the moment of her being ordered to his presence, no one expected any other result – for few possibly imagined, nor did the sultan himself, that she would have courage to brave the alternative rather than abandon the faith of her fathers. Such was the case.

She was first sent to Serail, where every means was employed to shake her constancy; threats, blandishments and the most brilliant promises were tried by turns and were equally unsuccessful. Even her relations were allowed to see her to endeavour by their persuasions to divert her from her resolution, but with a firmness which against such assaults could have been the effect only of the deepest conviction. This young and noble woman held fast her integrity and calmly chose a horrible though honourable death, to the enjoyment of an ignominious existence of shame and infamy.

The Jews came forward with offers of immense sums of money to save her but her fate was irrevocably decided and the only mercy the baffled tyrant could afford his young and innocent victim was to allow of her being decapitated instead of being burnt alive. I had an account of the closing scene from an eye witness who was one of the guards at the execution and although, as a body, there is nowhere a more dissolute set of irregular soldiery than the Moroccan Moors. He confessed to me that many of his vice hardened companions could not restrain their tears and that he himself could not look with dry eyes on a sight of such cold blooded atrocity.

This beautiful young woman was led out to where a pile of wood ready for firing had been raised for her last couch – her long dark hair flowing dishevelled over her shoulders; she looked around in vain for a heart and hand that could succour, though so many eyes pitied her. For the last time she was offered – with the executioner and the pyre in all their terror before her – her life, on condition of being false to her God. She only asked for a few minutes for prayer, after which her throat was cut by the executioner, according to the barbarous custom of the country and her body consumed on the fire!

Fellow countrymen! This is no Moorish romance, strained out of a heated imagination, to gratify the morbid taste of the fancy cloyed novel reader. There is no painting or exaggeration to excite false sympathy, just a simple tale of naked, un-varnished, thrilling truth. I appeal to you whether such things ought to be in the present age. I appeal to you whether such things ought to be allowed in a country where British influence can be brought to bear in the most remote manner, how much more in a country close to our shores? "We are verily guilty concerning our brother in that we saw the anguish of his soul when he besought us, and we would not hear".

It will scarcely be believed among us that all this contumely and insult, along with the most precarious tenure of property and life is called protection, and that for this so called protection a heavy annual poll tax is levied – yet such is the fact.

There is another situation to which this race is subjected – more frightful because more indiscriminate, affecting not only individuals, but the community. This is the periodical sack and plunder of their quarters whenever the reins of government are relaxed, either owing to civil dissension or local battles. The Jews, from the nature of their occupations as bankers, merchants and traders, and without the ability to buy land, accumulate large sums in bullion and often indulge their wives and adorn them with valuable jewellery. This naturally excites others into plundering the Jewish quarter whenever there is any hint of disturbance and unrest. How often have I heard their cries – the very people whose duty it is to guard the town are the first to begin the plunder. When it happens it looks like an enemy's town taken by storm.

In the event of any European power threatening them with chastisement for outrages on its subjects, the coast towers are immediately filled with black soldiery, country Moors and Arabs, as reinforcements; these pay little regard of obedience to their chiefs or governors and with the rabble of the towns are always meditating an onslaught on the Jewish quarter under pretext that if the infidels obtained the victory the Jews would rejoice at their disgrace and side with their enemies. Hence they anticipate their revenge while the poor Hebrews are still in their power. With such prospects around them it may be supposed in what constant terror this unfortunate race possess their lives and with what alarm they contemplate the possibility of civil disturbance or the approach of foreign enemies. Although often threatened, an interval of many years had elapsed since the last pillage of the quarter of the Jews at Mogadore, which I believe occurred during the confusion consequent upon the death of the late and the accession of the present sultan (but of this I am not certain) until the attack on the town by the French, when the Moors, smarting under their chastisement, gave vent to their fury on the defenceless Jews. The mind recoils with horror from the contemplation of the subsequent occurrences, aggravated as they were by the peculiar circumstance of the helplessness of their victims, we would therefore draw a veil over that which words can but faintly portray and at which the best feelings of our nature revolt.

Eminently blessed as we ourselves are by the mercy of God, it is difficult, nay almost impossible for us to realise a state of abasement so helpless, of degradation so extreme of civil destitution so complete as that to which this outcast people is reduced. We would rather believe that the statements are overdrawn than that such things exist at this late period of the Christian era. By cavilling at undeniable facts, we endeavour to shake off the fearful responsibility which they necessarily entail in our species.

If it is to be contended that the duty incumbent upon us to attempt a remedy of this crying evil is not a consequence of such conviction, let any free man, by a concentrated effort of abstraction of mind (and it requires an effort), place himself in the position of one of these outlaws of earth and if he do not abandon his argument I will not maintain their cause, but if, in this position, his flesh creep with horror and his blood boil with indignation at being stripped of his liberty and of everything which makes life dear to man and surrounded on all sides by insult, contumely and wrong, which it requires long training in servitude to endure with a show of patience, if he can then identify within himself the claim which this oppressed race has on his attention, his influence and his exertions, I call upon him by his gratitude for the great blessing he has received through the Jews, I call upon him for the sake of his own un-outraged domestic feelings, by his sympathy for the oppressed and by every cherished feeling as a man, a free man and above all a Christian man, to give me his aid in advocating the cause of these outcasts of Israel, and soliciting for them the beneficence of that nation whose soil gives freedom to the slave and at the same time affords an asylum to kings in their misfortunes – whose protecting sceptre rules with justice unparalleled over an empire which girds the earth, yet with the inconsistency of everything human, there is the greatest claim on their protection, there, alas! ... there is no help – at the foot of the British throne, were all nations find hope and succour, must the Israelite alone find neglect and despair?

Thoughts leading up to Edward's plan....

I shall now naturally be called upon and justly called upon, to point out some practicable means of encompassing the object I am so desirous of attaining. But before I develop the plan I have in view and which will take time for its accomplishment, I would propose, as a preliminary, that British influence should be exerted to ameliorate, in some degree the actual state of the Jews in every part of the world to which it can be effectually extended.

As respects Morocco, no time could be better chosen for the purpose than the present. The sultan and his Moslem subjects are more humbled into a due appreciation of the power of Christian states by the retribution lately inflicted upon them by the French. However this may have tended to endanger the peaceful relations of Europe and have been looked on with a jealous eye in England, it was justly incurred by a long course of accumulated wrong and insult not only towards the French themselves, but towards every nation of Christendom, whose flag they have insulted and whose power they have defied. (Will it be believed that up to this time, Sweden and Denmark paid an annual tribute in hard cash to this despicable state, and the large presents constantly sent them by the English Government were also looked on by them in the same light. It cannot, therefore be wondered at, that their pride was inflated and their insolence unbounded.) Let it, therefore, now be known among them that England takes an interest in the welfare of this nation, and though it may excite their surprise, it will arrest their attention and induce their forbearance.

That there is a disposition on the part of our government, to answer every appeal in favour of the unprotected and the wronged, there can be no doubt and I turn with complacency to the noble stand made by our ministers on the late occasion of the executions in Turkey of Christian apostates from Islamism, when with undaunted magnanimity the British government pledged its integrity and perilled the peace of Europe on the event – and succeeded, how could it fail? – in gaining their point though wrested from the Turks at the sacrifice of the fundamental doctrines of Islamism. See despatch sent by Earl of Aberdeen to Sir J Canning in the Appendix I page 45.

By interfering in their behalf and thus gradually giving ease to the galling yoke of Arab bondage under which they groan, we may bring out the peculiar constitutional elasticity of the Jewish temperament and prepare them without premature haste and without fear of the sudden revulsion which would be the effect of more decided measures for their eventual deliverance from the land of their captivity and the full enjoyment of freedom and independence.

I have alluded more particularly in this imperfect sketch, to the Jews of Morocco, because they are essentially the most ill-used and because – although I have had opportunities of seeing much of this people in that country as well as Turkey, Syria, Palestine, India and Arabia, I consider them physically and intellectually as the finest type of the race and their apparent moral degradation is chiefly superficial, the consequence of the state of oppression which has been weighing on them for nearly 2000 years. I am prepared in advocating their cause for the smile of incredulity and the scoff of ridicule from those who form their opinion of the Hebrew people from the denizens of Monmouth Street and who might, with equal justice, derive materials for their estimate of the British character from the inhabitants of the collieries or the purlieus of St Giles's. They cannot believe that any good qualities can pertain to this proscribed and despised nation, and yet in a late publication, some startling facts are collected and combined, and assisted by much conjecture, to prove that the Anglo-Saxons are of the Israelitish stock and origin.

Were the proofs of this more unanswerable, it would not be matter of regret, but the contrary, as there is nothing derogatory in partaking of the noblest blood in the world, and it would moreover be of great service in abrogating those prejudices which are the greatest obstacles to any effort being made to relieve this people from their present unfortunate position. It is not, indeed, surprising that after the ordeal they have undergone, they should still retain either moral worth or physical identity, yet not withstanding this, which would have utterly annihilated any race not equally the care of Providence, there are still among them men of latent talent and capability for the highest purposes and which only require directing into the right channels to produce the most brilliant results. They possess in an eminent degree the virtues of fortitude and perseverance, without which indeed they could scarcely have existed individually or held together as a nation. Their aspirations after better things have been quelled, their spirit bowed to the very dust and their every feeling embittered under the thraldom of Mohammedan despotism, the persecution of the powers of Christendom and the insults of the world at large. But relieved from these fetters, the intrinsic nobility of their nature would be drawn forth and springing with their characteristic buoyancy from the sufferings of ages, they would reach and maintain a high rank among the nations of the earth.

Edward's plan for the re-establishment of the Jewish nation...

The plan I would now propose is, first, the re-establishment of the Jewish nation in Palestine as a protected state, under the guardianship of Great Britain, during a period to be regulated by their advances towards the present state of knowledge and enlightened civilization.

Secondly, their final establishment as an independent state when so ever the parent institutions shall have acquired sufficient force and vigour to allow of this tutelage being withdrawn and the national character shall be sufficiently recovered from its depression to allow of their governing themselves.

This proposition will hardly be considered visionary, while it would be highly beneficial to the Jewish people, and would be attended with political advantages of incalculable importance to Great Britain, tending to restore the balance of her power in the Middle East, and giving her the command of free and uninterrupted communication with the East.

In consideration of a subject of this nature, it is impossible to lose sight of the position of Russia in the Middle East or to be blind to the quiet encroaching policy of our now friendly ally. She does not colonise but absorbs – she does not naturalise individuals, but nations. Let us take a retrospective glance – Poland, Ingria, Livonia, Courland, Krim, Tartary, Kabarda, Mingrelia are Russian. She has absorbed Finland, Bessarabia, Inneritia and the territory from the shores of the Caspian (to the whole of which sea she asserts her right) to the frontiers of China, but what more regards our present subject is, that after overflowing and Russianising Georgia, she has passed the river Aras and confidently anticipates the annexation of the rich countries of Asia Minor, part of which (Armenia) she overran and retired from, the state of her relations, with the great powers of Europe not allowing the consummation of so daring a step.

On the other hand we have France and Algeria and I do not hesitate to assert, that in the event of anything arising to disturb the present peaceful aspect of affairs, our communication with India and China etc, is not safe for a single day. On what does its supposed safety depend? The goodwill of a worn out old man? It may possibly be his successor's interest or policy to continue the same friendly dispositions, but such friendship is very precarious and always bestowed by these mercenary states on the strongest in any struggle.

Can we trust Turkey? It cannot protect itself and is crumbling to ruin from foundation to battlement. It is unworthy of a power like Great Britain, on whose vigour and integrity the peace and happiness of so many nations and the very existence of some, depends, to allow one of the most vital arteries of her system remaining unprotected from enemies, or at the mercy of doubtful friends. When foreign influence in Egypt on a late occasion attempted to tamper with this essential spring of strength, it caused a thrill of alarm and indignation throughout the British Empire. No, we must have our own protection in our own hands and we could not employ better means for securing this object than the instrumentality of a people of sufficient abilities to act under good counsels and united among themselves by every tie of religion, patriotism and nationality.

The re-establishment of the Jewish nation in Palestine under British protection, would retrieve our affairs in the Middle East and place us in a commanding position from whence to check the progress of encroachment, to overawe open enemies and if necessary to repel their advance – at the same time that it would place the management of our steam communication entirely in our own hands.

There would probably be little difficulty in negotiating a treaty with Turkey for the cession of the territory required for the purpose, but should there be any objection on their part, the advantages which would accrue to all parties are so great and the importance of the measure to the interests of civilization and humanity is so immense, that we should be prepared, even in common justice, to take possession of it for the proposed object aim at once.

Setting boundaries for the new State...

The boundaries of the land can only, at present, be laid down by approximation, but the most advantageous limits should be the result of special observation and ulterior inquiry. It does not appear necessary, however, that it should extend towards the **NORTH,** far beyond the town of Acre, the limit being a line drawn from the vicinity of the waters of Merom to the sea coast. With the fortress of Acre open to succours from the sea, this frontier would be impregnable. The boundary on the **EAST** should be a line on the eastern bank of the Jordan, the lake of Tiberias and the Dead Sea. It would be requisite to establish a chain of small forts or blockhouses on the whole of this line, they should occupy commanding situations to keep in check the various tribes of predatory Arabs, with whom no alliance would be of any validity or duration, unless backed by power at hand to chastise its infraction or unless their forbearance was purchased. But such a course is at all times dishonourable and I have witnessed so much of the ruinous effects of this system (see Note 2 on page 41) in Afghanistan, that I would ever deprecate a recurrence to it.

The **SOUTHERN** boundary is not easy to define without personal inspection as it must border on the desert. But the **WESTERN** boundary, besides the Mediterranean, should be continued by a line from the sea coast to the head of the Gulf of Suez. The possession of Suez would be immaterial, as a station equally eligible might be easily found on the eastern shore of the gulf as an emporium and resort for Indian steamers, the more so, as Suez obtains its supply of water from the east coast. As soon as an advantageous position can be fixed on for a corresponding sea port in the Mediterranean, either at El Arish, Gaza, Jaffa or elsewhere, the whole of European steamers should be removed from the present inconvenient port of Alexandria, and no time should be lost in running a railway between the two stations, pending which the communication could be carried on by the ordinary means.

Let us only contemplate for a moment the confusion of our affairs consequent upon the breaking up of our transit arrangement through Egypt, a contingency which may happen at any day or any hour and we shall be convinced that this indispensible link is still wanting to the chain of Great Britain's powers as well as safety.

The question here arises, how are the current nomadic tribes of this area to be relocated? If the people settled within these boundaries were of the sedentary nature of Europeans, or possessed any feeling of attachment to the soil, I acknowledge this would offer some difficulty, but when we consider that they are races essentially nomadic and migratory, the difficulties disappear. During the supremacy of Mohammed Ali in Palestine, the Arab had almost everywhere superseded the Turkish race, now, probably, (for I have not visited these countries since they were restored to the Porte), the Turks may again be resuming the preponderance, for the two people do not coalesce, a lasting antipathy subsisting between them. The country, compared with its extent, is at present thinly populated, yet the pressure caused by the introduction of so large a body of strangers upon the actual inhabitants might be attended with injurious results. Before, however, attempting to make a settlement, it would be desirable that the country should be prepared for their reception. This might be done by inducing the Turkish government to make the present Arab inhabitants fall back upon the extensive and partially cultivated countries of Asia Minor, where they might be put in possession of tracts and allocations, equally advantageous and far superior in value to those they abandoned. Although this proposition may not be consistent with the spirit of our institutions, it is consistent with the arbitrary manners and customs of these Orientals with whom such things are of frequent occurrence and it would be attended with little hardship to a migratory people who consider themselves strangers in the land and whose entire movables consist of a carpet and a few cooking utensils. There still remains the Christian population, these are thinly scattered through the various towns with the exception of Bethlehem and Nazareth, whose inhabitants are nearly all of that faith. The Syrian Christians are ignorant and superstitious and the position in which the Jews would be placed with respect to them might therefore appear likely to lead to collisions unfavourable to their peaceful settlement. But in fact there is little danger to be apprehended, for these Christians are themselves helpless and require protection – and harmless except when made the instruments of persecution by bigoted and designing Europeans.

I had an opportunity of seeing an instance of this at Damascus, on the occasion of the disappearance of a monk belonging to the Capuchin convent. For the purpose of raising a persecution against the Jews, they were reported to have made away with him – this false pretext was soon magnified into the general accusation of child murder, and shameful to say, this malicious attempt at reviving the worn out superstitions of Europe, against a harmless and defenceless race, (see Note 3 on page 43) was headed and fomented by the consul of civilized France, Mr Rattimenton and the European monks.

But for the uncalled for interference of these persons, the original cause of the disturbance could have been the subject only of a few days wonder, for want of even the slightest circumstantial evidence to bring home a crime to anyone, much less to the object of their fanatical animosity. A persecution was, never the less raised against them, severe, though necessarily of short duration, for as soon as it became known, it was put down by the indignation of Europe.

Such things in the present day could happen only under an Arab government and I mention it to show that the Christian population are not themselves disposed to initiate disturbances and to prevent their becoming the tools of others, a very temperate exercise of authority would be required.

Every conciliatory measure consistent with firmness might be extended to them and the several Christian powers, under whose protection the convents now existing, are professedly placed, should be applied to, to furnish them with good, intelligent and peaceful superiors. These convents should not be allowed to acquire more property in land than they already possess, and all, whether ecclesiastical or civil, be made strictly amenable to the laws which might be framed to regulate the new state.

I avoid entering on the very wide question of the conversion of the Jews as being quite foreign to the subject in its political bearings – but speaking from personal observation, I do not apprehend that they would evince any disposition to revert to the forms of their abrogated dispensation – for however averse to enquiry and fearful of looking fairly into the subject, men of intelligence among them (and with these we should have to deal) feel and cannot conceal from themselves, that the time for such things is irretrievably past – besides which, it should be made an indispensable condition of our assistance, that they should not attempt to restore their obsolete ceremonial.

Every important enterprise must necessarily be attended with some difficulty. Many impediments which in the distant perspective appear dangerous or immoveable, when boldly approached, diminish gradually and disappear. I would anticipate every possible objection to the carrying out of this project, but after considerably weighing all that can be alleged against it, I find nothing which an ordinary share of judgement and resolution may not easily surmount and remove.

Supposing therefore, the country placed at our disposal, with these or similar boundaries, we must now take into consideration the amount of force which would be required for its protection. Having little military experience, anything I may propose on this head can only be by way of suggestion and may be improved on, or set aside altogether, by superior professional skill. I consider then, that three subsidiary regiments of infantry, two of irregular cavalry and twelve field pieces, would be an adequate force to maintain the peace of the interior and the integrity of the frontier, so far as native hostility is concerned. But should this be thought too small for the purpose, it should be borne in mind that it is free from the very great objections applicable to a larger force – which are, the want of rapidity of movement, the superior difficulty of obtaining supplies and the rash confidence generated by numbers, by which the results of so many arduous undertakings have been sacrificed.

Defence & protection –
Northern, Middle and Southern Provinces...

For the proper distribution of this force, as well as for important general purposes, this territory should be divided into **three provinces**, unequal in extent, but regard being had to the general aspect of the country (See map on page 39).

The **Northern Province**, being mountainous, should have for its southern boundary a line drawn diagonally from the sea coast, south of Mount Carmel to the river Jordan. To this division should be allotted one regiment of foot and a brigade of six guns; head-quarters at Acre, with detachments at Tiberias, Nazareth and Jenin.

The **Midland Province**, likewise mountainous, should be separated from the southern by a line from Gaza, running south of Bethlehem, to the Dead Sea. One regiment of infantry would suffice for this province, to be stationed at Nablous, with detachments at Jaffa, Jerusalem and Jericho.

The **Southern Province**, being flatter, verging on the desert and affording greater facilities of transport, would comprise a larger extent and reach to the borders of Egypt. This province should have the third regiment of foot and a brigade of six guns – head-quarters at Hebron, with detachments at Gazza, El Arish and the new station on the Red Sea. In this division should also be the head quarters of the two bodies of irregular horse. These should be raised from the Arabs of the bordering tribes, to be employed chiefly for the protection of the overland mail route, besides being available for the other provinces and especially for their eastern frontier.

The bay of Acre might be made the station, during the favourable season for part of the Mediterranean fleet and it would be very desirable to place a small armed iron steamer on the Dead Sea.

The country once settled, agriculture and commerce would naturally follow from the genial influence of British protection – I speak from personal observation of the effect of the mere influence of the English name in the neighbourhood of Herat in 1841 (see Note 4 on page 43), where, from this avowed protection alone, the whole country was fast recovering from the devastation and desolation caused by the unprincipled tyranny of its rulers and the people returning to the peaceful occupation of trade and cultivation and where the existence of a British tappal station, without even the presence of an European, was sufficient to rally cultivators around it and redeem the country from sterility. Alas, that such fair prospects should been so early blighted and such advantages so disgracefully sacrificed! But why it may be asked, when on the threshold of a new enterprise, recall the discouraging retrospect of past disasters? Because it is the part of true courage, not only to be daunted by failure, but to investigate with unshrinking mind the causes and remote springs of past misfortunes, in order to guard against their recurrence. We won not that land by our own sword – and its loss was the consequence and punishment of the vices of its invaders (see Note 5 and latter part of Note 2 on page 44) and the abuse of their advantages. (A tappal station is a place for delivery and collection of post).

A judicial blindness rendered them totally unconscious of the dangers that surrounded them and when the blow fell, the paralyzed energies of the mass could oppose little resistance to the storm brought on by the culpable incapacity of its leaders. When we divest ourselves of the trammels of prejudice and soar above the political atmosphere, it is impossible not to be struck, as we look down with unclouded eye on all the jarring elements, which rack and toss individuals and nations in the action and reaction of the conflict of good and evil – it is impossible not to be struck with the conviction of an irresistibly overruling influence co-existing with the entire free will of man, but directing his councils to the ends of Providence.

Where the councils of man are in accordance with the will of God, they are superabundantly blessed and issue in results most glorious; but where the contrary, either the evil which would end in ruin is mercifully warded off, or the most magnificent undertakings of the pride of man, - the toilsome fruit of master-minds and the labour of million hands, are suddenly blighted by one breath of the angel of death or shattered by the blast of the ireful elements asserting the majesty of the Eternal, in calm derision of the unhallowed efforts of his creatures. The present however, is in no respect a parallel case, besides which, instead of the direction of affairs being in the hands of a secondary agent, a demoralised government, it would be under the immediate and vigilant guidance of the British cabinet itself.

Palestine, though now barren and desolate, requires only an active and industrious population, so abundant are its natural advantages of soil and climate to restore its original fertility. Not only is it rich in the indigenous produce of the Middle East, it is equally adapted to the productions of Europe and the tropics. Commerce from these circumstances alone must spring into life. But when we consider the known wealth of the Jews and the immense funds they could command, together with the financial and mercantile experience which they would bring with them on their return to the land of their fathers, what a magnificent prospect of commerce is spread before us – what an extensive market for our manufactures! With this disposition of the Jews, engrafted on them by the habits of centuries and judicious encouragement, this protected state might in a few years monopolise the whole import trade of Central Asia and compete with the commerce of Russia on its own southern frontier.

The advantages derivable to England from this measure are so great that it would almost appear that my real object was to benefit my own country, instead of advocating the cause of a proscribed and harmless race, but so true is it, that "Cast thy bread upon the waters and it shall return to thee after many days" that the protection afforded to these people would quickly return in blessings on England, and be felt in the wretched hearts and homes of the poor manufacturers of Manchester, Birmingham and Glasgow.

It is not supposed that the British government require any inducement to the undertaking of so noble a work of humanity, when once convinced of its feasibility and the probability of its success, that we would recapitulate the advantages to be derived from it. But we would speak to the public mind – not only those persons to whom great and good actions are their own recommendation, but those also whose opinions and judgements are governed by interest and expediency only in the adoption of any proposed political measures. It is therefore, that we would point out the vast advantages to our commerce and manufactures, the safety attendant on securing our overland communication in our own hands and the most important bulwarks against national enemies, from this desirable footing in the Middle East, all insured by this step, as well as the ulterior cheering prospects of the spirit of religion and civilization which it promises.

The Jews in all parts of the world have, during the lapse of years, kept their attention and hopes fixed on Palestine, to which country they never doubt of returning. Large collections in money are annually made throughout all the countries where they are numerous and willingly given for the support of the synagogue at Jerusalem. They would eagerly embrace the opportunity offered them of returning thither, and their gratitude to their deliverers would be unbounded at the same time that they could attain no good end by turning against us.

Although, as already mentioned, this subject has been more forcibly impressed on my mind by their persecutions and sufferings, which have induced me to lift up a voice in their behalf, the condition of this extraordinary race of people has long been to me a consideration of deep sympathy and absorbing interest and I cannot but entertain the conviction that whether we hear or whether we forbear, something of the nature of the arrangements herein proposed, must take place at some early period. For thus saith the Lord, which giveth the sun for a light by day and the ordinances of the moon and stars for a light by night. If those ordinances depart before me, then the seed of Israel also shall cease from being a nation before me forever. I will lift up my hand to the gentiles and set up my standard to the people and they shall bring thy sons in their arms and thy daughters shall be carried on their shoulders. I will take the children of Israel from among the heathen whither they be gone and will gather them on every side and bring them into their own land and they shall dwell in the land that I have given unto Jacob my servant, *wherein your fathers have dwelt* and they shall dwell therein, even *they and their children* and their *children's children* for ever, and they shall say "This land that *was desolate is become* like the garden of Eden, and the waste and desolate and ruined cities are become fenced and are inhabited."

Edward L Mitford
Colombo, March 1845

MITFORD LITERARY SOCIETY

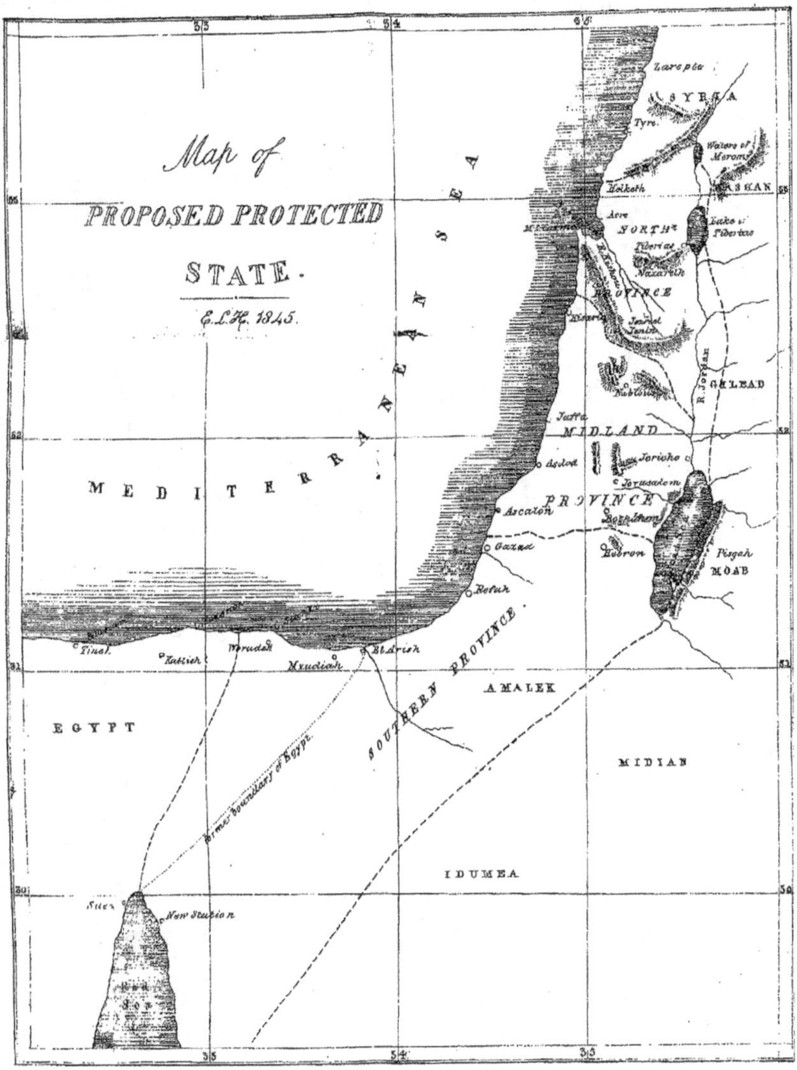

MAP OF PROPOSED
PROTECTED STATE OF ISRAEL
Hand drawn by Edward Ledwich Mitford 1845

MITFORD LITERARY SOCIETY

NOTES – 1

We were now in Koordistan and the guide having put us on the track which led to Zacu, begged to be allowed to return and we accordingly dismissed him. The road lay for some distance along the left bank of the Tigris before entering the mountains. The weather and scenery were both fine and we found ourselves riding entirely alone, without escort or protection, in a country and place always considered impassable on account of the lawless character of the local people. I could not help observing to my companion, that the so called millennium appeared to already begin. (Edward's companion would later become Sir Austen Henry Layard, Under Secretary of State for Foreign Affairs).

The inhabitants of this and other countries which we have traversed without inconvenience or molestation must either have been much belied by former visitors, or a most extraordinary spirit of peace and goodwill has since diffused itself over these regions to create such a change in their natures. Before I had an opportunity of judging for myself, I had been led to imagine that the Turks were brutal, the Albanians sanguinary and as for the Koords, nothing was too bad to say of them. I was therefore, agreeably surprised to find the Turks courteous and urbane, the Albanians, though far from heros of romance, plain soldiers and harmless if uninjured, and the Koords hospitable and good natured.

Had these people deserved the evil reports brought up against them, there was nothing to prevent their making away with solitary travellers like ourselves with the utmost impunity, in the wild district between this, Zacu and beyond. Their subjection to Turkey is only nominal and what revenue they pay is more in form of a tribute than a regular tax. These mountaineers would not have much respect for a sultan's firman, if indeed men were in the habit of asking for your passport before robbing you; but I am proud to think that the name and undisguised profession of an Englishman is a more powerful protection and safeguard in all the countries where we are not actually at war, than any countenance of the local authorities and this feeling it ought always to be the object of a traveller to cultivate.
Reference – ELM travel notes 6 April 1840.

NOTES – 2

Yar Mohammed is only prevented from openly avowing his hostility to the English by the fear of losing the large sums of money which he is constantly receiving from the Indian government. This payment of money is openly wasted, for should we stop these supplies or experience any reverse, he will throw off the mask and reveal his true colours, by acting against us. The use of money for the furtherance of our political views in these countries is carried to disgraceful extremes. One chief, who has it in his power to offer us opposition by his situation amongst fortresses and knowledge of the country and encouraged by our backwardness in drawing him from his retreat and destroying his power, is bought off, by a monthly or yearly stipend or bribe, as a reward for his forbearance.

A neighbouring chief, hitherto quiet, relying on our supineness, and the prospect of similar advantages, immediately arms against us, cuts off our supplies, molests our marches and makes himself troublesome enough to be bought off and pensioned in his turn and this goes on successively one after another and requires very little discernment to see that wherever we stop our pay, we have established a enemy conscious of his power until eventually every leader of any spirit has become our pensioner and despises us for our cowardice.

It may answer very well to pension imbecile princes whose dominions we have taken possession of, or traitor ministers who have assisted us in our views, but buying off hill tribes and robber chiefs is like pouring water into a sieve – it counteracts its own purpose, promotes opposition and buys us enemies when it might be turned to much better account in other ways.

(Prince Kamran had handed over the actual day to day administration of Herat to Wazir Yar Muhammad Khan who apparently, later assassinated him in 1841, and took over the throne of Herat).

Reference – ELM travels in Afghanistan, October 1840.

I have before noticed with reprobation the system of making war with gold. It is the byword of every Afghan. Show them a Bukkur, Guzni, Cabool or Kelaat and they answer "Your money gained them, not your arms". And they are not far wrong in detecting the general practice. The Afghans, and especially the hill tribes, when compared with other Asiatics, are a warlike people – they have been gradually recovering from the panic caused by our sudden invasion and finding that the only weapon we are now willing to employ is gold – they take advantage of our want of spirit to enrich themselves. Forgetting that our difficulties were only beginning after our occupation – a body of officials were thrown into this country without sufficient regard to their diplomatic capabilities, an indiscriminate selection being made, guided chiefly by interest; some few clever men were necessarily included, but from accident rather than discrimination on the part of those who appointed them.

These political agents, highly paid and bewildered by their sudden accession of good fortune and importance, engrossed by their public and private state and abandoned to luxury and display, were not likely to command the respect of the people. Supplies of money were lavishly poured into the hands of these agents and as lavishly distributed to the Afghans, buying at the same time their forbearance and their contempt – they receive our money, despise our agents and almost doubt whether their enemies are Englishmen. And thus are our military reputation and moral influence uselessly sacrificed, whilst from Cabul to Herat, from Herat to Scinde, nothing is now heard of but bad policy, mismanagement and ruin.

Reference – ELM travels in Afghanistan & Scinde 24 February 1841.

NOTES – 3

Thomas Percy makes the following pertinent remarks on the ballad of the Jew's Daughter, in his Reliques of Ancient Poetry. This ballad is founded upon the supposed practice of the Jews in crucifying, or otherwise murdering Christian children, out of hatred to the religion of their parents, a practice which has been always acknowledged in excuse for the cruelties exercised upon that wretched people, but which probably never happened in a single instance; For if we consider, on the one hand, the ignorance and superstition of the times when such stories took their rise, the virulent prejudices of the monks who record them and the eagerness with which they would be catched up by the barbarous populace as a pretence for plunder – on the other hand, the great danger incurred by the perpetrators and the inadequate motives they could have to excite to a crime of so much horror, we may reasonably conclude the whole charge to be groundless and malicious.
Reference - Thomas Percy (1729-1811) Ballad of the Jew's Daughter, in his Reliques of Ancient Poetry, Vol 1 page 35 published in 1764.

NOTES – 4

The British envoy arrived at Herat in August 1839, since when a great change has been effected. The town has revived from its ashes, the population has returned, the peasantry are restoring their villages and resuming the cultivation of their lands and caravans of Herattees are continually arriving from Mushed and other places to which they had fled for refuge and re-occupying their deserted homes under the protection of the English name. 28 Oct 1840.

A quarter of a mile beyond the little river of Adruscund (western Afghanistan) is a small enclosure, thirty-two yards square, built by us as a tappal station and where forage and rice is procurable. This valley was a year ago abandoned but has now quite revived, owing, as the inhabitants assert, to British protection. Several villages, surrounded by cultivation, now line the banks of the stream. What an exhibition is this of the effect of moral influence in promoting the most desirable ends. The mere establishment of a small English tappal station is such an evidence of confidence in our own power in the eyes of the natives, as to induce them to settle round the spot, to build villages, dig canals and cultivate their fields. I have long been convinced that if we had established clever and accredited agents throughout these countries, such a system would have obviated the necessity of our present expensive military occupation. The time for this is now past. We have sown the wind and I hope we may not reap the whirlwind.

Reference – ELM travels in Afghanistan, 9 November 1840.

NOTES – 5

I am sorry to say that a great deal of the ill-feeling in the minds of the natives of Afghanistan towards us has been generated by the unrestrained licence of many of our own people. If all that I have heard be true, they have been much outraged on a point on which all Muslims are particularly sensitive and vulnerable. It was a common complaint among them and I was much struck by a remark which was made by a man of rank in Kandahar to one of our political agents – "You Feringees", he said, "are not content with taking our country, our towns and property, but you will not leave us even our wives". I remarked at the time, that was it possible these people should ever gain the ascendant, or ever have us in their power; they would exact a fearful vengeance. The depravity of the people themselves is no excuse for us – they will bear with much from their own rulers which they will not endure from a Frank and a Christian. If Englishmen as a body lose that high tone of moral feeling and the greatness of soul which has raised the British nation to its present glorious pre-eminence, their physical power will avail them little, but, on the contrary, precipitate their downfall.

Reference – ELM travels in Afghanistan 20 Nov 1840.

APPENDIX 1

Copy of Dispatch from the Earl of Aberdeen
(Secretary of State for Foreign Affairs)
to Sir Stratford Canning, H.M. Ambassador at Constantinople.
(From the Despatches laid before Parliament by H.M. command)

Foreign Office, 16th January 1844.

Sir,
I have received your Excellency's dispatch of the 17th of December, reporting that a Greek had been executed near Broussa, as an apostate from Islamism and enclosing a copy of the communication which you had directed Mr Dragoman Pisani to make to the Porte (the central government of the Ottoman Empire), in consequence of this transaction. But the repetition of a scene of this revolting kind, so soon after that which had, in the course of last summer, excited the horror and indignation of Europe, evinces such total disregard on the part of the Porte, for the feelings and remonstrance's of the Christian powers, that it is incumbent upon H.M.'s government, without loss of time, to convey their sentiments on the matter still more explicitly to the knowledge of the Porte.

They take this course singly and without waiting for the cooperation of the other Christian powers because they desire to announce to the Porte, a determination, which though it doubtless will be concurred in by all, Great Britain is prepared to act upon alone. HM's government feel too, that they have an especial right to require to be listened to by the Porte in a matter of this nature, for they can appeal to the justice and to the favour with which the vast body of Arabs, subject to the British rule, are treated in India, in support of their demand, that all persons, subjects of the Porte and professing Christianity, shall be exempt from cruel and arbitrary persecution on account of their religion and shall not be made the victims of a barbarous law, which it may be sought to enforce for their destruction.

Whatever may have been tolerated in former times by the weakness of indifference of Christian powers, those powers will now require from the Porte due consideration for their feelings, as members of a religious community, and interested as such in the fate of all, who notwithstanding shades of difference, unite in a common belief in the essential doctrines of Christianity; and they will not endure that the Porte should insult and trample on their faith by treating as a criminal any person who embraces it. HM's government require the Porte to abandon, once for all, so revolting a principle.

They have no wish to humble the Porte by imposing upon it an unreasonable obligation, but as a Christian government, the protection of those who profess common belief with themselves, from persecution and oppression, on that account alone, by their Arab rulers, is a paramount duty with them and one from which they cannot recede.

Your Excellency will therefore press upon the Turkish government, that if the Porte has any regards for the friendship of England – if it has any hope that in the hour of peril or of adversity, that protection, which has more than once saved it from destruction, will be extended to it again, it must renounce absolutely, and without equivocation, the barbarous practice which has called forth the remonstrance now addressed to it.

Your Excellency will require an early answer and you will let the Turkish ministers understand, that if that answer does not fully correspond with expectations which HM's government entertain, your Excellency is instructed to seek audience of the sultan and to explain to H. Highness in the most forcible terms, the feelings of the British government and the consequences, so injurious to Turkey, which a disregard for those feelings will involve.

HM's government are so anxious for the continuance of a good understanding with Turkey, and that the Porte should entitle itself to their good offices in the hour of need, that they wish to leave no expedient untried before they shall be compelled to admit the conviction that all their interest and friendship is misplaced, and that nothing remains for them but to look forward to, if not promote, the arrival of the day, when the force of circumstances shall bring about a change, which they will have vainly hoped to procure, from the prudence and humanity of the Porte itself.

Your Excellency will seek an interview with the Reis Effendi, and having read to him this despatch; leave a copy of it, with an accurate translation, in his hands.
(Signed Aberdeen, Secretary of State for Foreign Affairs)

APPENDIX 2

Since writing these pages I have seen a pamphlet by Mr A Anderson, recommending the restoration of the canal from Suez to Pelusium. This proposition was considered of sufficient importance to be published in papers laid before Parliament by HM's command. Should this be found as practicable as is there asserted, it would be advisable to include the latter place, now called Tineh, within the boundary of the new state herein proposed.

In the same publication occur the following remarks, with which I will conclude. "The communications by this route have, however, already become of sufficient magnitude and importance to render any measure calculated to ensure their permanency and security, deserving of the serious attention of the government, and of the active solicitude of the public, both of this country and of India.

Edward L Mitford
Colombo, March 1845

MITFORD LITERARY SOCIETY

With kind thanks to the University of Edinburgh

MITFORD LITERARY SOCIETY

THE MITFORD DYNASTY

A true story. The book covers 33 generations of the Mitford family from 1042 to the 21st century. Set in the village of Mitford, Northumberland & Hunmanby and Filey Bay in Yorkshire, the greater part of the activity takes part during the Victorian era and going with current trends would provide excellent material for a television series as filmed in the village itself that was owned by the lords and squires of Mitford for the past 960 years, which includes Mitford Castle, Mitford Manor, Mitford Hall, Mitford Church, Mitford Chapel and the village of Mitford.

From the words, carved into the stone wall of Mitford Castle dungeon, "Captivus Morior 141" (Captive I Die)..... to the gallant support of Roger Bertram to force King John to sign the Magna Carta at Runnymede in 1215, only to have Mitford village and church burnt with all the villagers inside – the Mitford dynasty continued its never ending saga and adventure from the beginning of England and British Empire to a dismal ending of perfect indifference in the 21st century.

From establishing the first hospital on the subcontinent of India (Mitford Hospital, Dhaka, Bangladesh) to the very heart and soul of British culture and politics in London. John Mitford edited and published the works of English poets, Milton, Swift, Parnell, Young, Lamb, Wordsworth, Byron and Gray. Edward Mitford FRGS, specialist on the Middle East was the first person to ride 10,000 miles on horseback through 16 countries from London to Ceylon (now Sri Lanka). Bertram Mitford FRGS, a founder of South African literature, was the first person to travel around South Africa to interview the survivors of the Zulu War at Isandlwana, the worst defeat of the British during the Victorian era. He then wrote 43 bestselling novels covering the history and culture of South Africa. From Europe to the Middle East and Africa, to Japan and China, Australia and New Zealand, you'll find the name Mitford.

Many have heard of the six Mitford girls. Nancy, the novelist (Love in a Cold Climate) Pamela, an excellent cook and farmer, Diana, who married Bryan Guinness, heir to the Guinness brewery fortune and two years later married Sir Oswald Mosley, the fascist leader. Due to their admiration of Hitler, they got locked up in Holloway Prison for three years. Unity, became a friend of Hitler and Nazi supporter and shot herself when war was declared between England and Germany; Jessica, became a communist and writer and emigrated to America, and Deborah – became Duchess of Devonshire and Chatsworth, last of the Mitford girls. Thomas, their only brother, was killed in Burma.

Friends have often quipped, synonymous with the name Mitford, is the word... scandal. True. It would appear that the family is quite practised at creating scandals, since 1215, in fact. However, this book is not about the Mitford girls. They are a branch of the original family. Undoubtedly they make interesting reading, however, it's the original mainline Mitford family that provides the truly fascinating and amazing story.

Today, from family archives, South African born Hugh Mitford Raymond, great-great grandson, nephew and cousin to the last seven squires of Mitford since 1042, presents the untold story of the Mitford family of Mitford, Northumberland. The estate was sold as no heir could be found and the dynasty ended with the death of the last squire in 2002. If you enjoy true life history, read the facts and events leading up the tragic ending of nearly 1000 years of family heritage along with the intrigue, betrayal and all that goes with the real thing - you be the judge? To quote the words inscribed on his great-great grandfather's gravestone in Mitford churchyard "There the tears of earth are dried – there the hidden things are clear". Edward Mitford FRGS, 27th Squire of Mitford.

To be published in 2016

www.facebook.com/mitforddynasty